A publication of the
**National Wildfire
Coordinating Group**

Clinical Treatment Guidelines for Wildland Fire Medical Units

PMS 551

July 2012

Clinical Treatment Guidelines for Wildland Fire Medical Units

July 2012

PMS 551

Sponsored for NWCG publication by the NWCG Risk Management Committee. Prepared and maintained by the Incident Emergency Medical Subcommittee (IEMS). Questions regarding the content of this product should be directed to subcommittee at BLM_FA_NWCG_IEMS@blm.gov.

This product is available electronically at: http://www.nwcg.gov.

Previous editions: none.

Contents

Tables

Preface

In 2010, the Incident Emergency Medical Subcommittee (IEMS), operating under the authority of the National Wildfire Coordinating Group (NWCG) - Risk Management Committee, completed the document, *Interim Minimum Standards for Medical Units Managed By NWCG Member Agencies*. The document was the first of several to be developed that will address the need for uniform standards and safe delivery of medical care provided by Emergency Medical Services (EMS) personnel at wildland fire. It focused on recognizing current practices and recommending standards to medical units for; promoting the use of licensed personnel within their scope of practice, state EMS office notification, applicable rules and jurisdictions, medical direction, communications, patient transportation and medical equipment, medication and supplies used.

The IEMS also committed to developing wildland fire specific protocols and this document, *Clinical Treatment Guidelines for Wildland Fire Medical Units*, PMS 551, is the finished product. A task group of physicians with diverse backgrounds in wildland fire medicine, wilderness medicine and emergency/ clinical backgrounds reviewed this document and provided valuable input. These guidelines where developed with the expectation that the typical appropriate Basic Life Support (BLS) or Advanced Life Support (ALS) EMS interventions will be provided as needed so we did not include detailed protocols for EMS medical or trauma patient care, which already exists. Rather, we focused on guidance for the unique differences and challenges associated with remote sites and expanded evaluation skills needed for patient care issues such as:

1) assisting a patient with first aid and self-care health management;
2) triaging conditions for recognition of appropriate self-care assistance vs. need for transport to clinical medical care; and
3) initiating urgent/EMS care using appropriate and predetermined transport modes.

Clinical Treatment Guidelines for Wildland Fire Medical Units was developed using categories by body system or specific body part along with the most common environmental emergencies seen during fire incidents. Each body system, body part or environmental emergency included begins with the boxed header of "**Triage Priority**". The following four conditions are used to determine when and with what degree of urgency a patient transport occurs if one or more of the bulleted qualifying criteria are present:

Emergency Condition- Transport patient by most rapid, appropriate method available to definitive emergency medical care

Urgent Condition – Hospital Evaluation is necessary, ambulance transport as needed

Semi-Urgent Condition – Physician evaluation is necessary, timeline recommendation for semi-urgent is that day, within 8-10 hours or first thing the next morning

Routine Condition – Medical Unit may provide access to over the counter medications, diet or fluid recommendations, first aid care and remedies

Before using these guidelines EMS personnel must be aware that state regulations, an on-site physician, on-line medical control or off-line directives from a medical director with jurisdiction may supersede these guidelines. Additionally, supplemental training of EMS personnel will be necessary in the areas of over the counter medications, clinical evaluations, patient reassessment, and diagnostic equipment. Any supplemental training should meet respective state or local regulations and policy.

Finally, considerations for multiple patients with potentially contagious diseases and integration of services with federal, state, tribal and local public health officials may become necessary.

IEMS continues to support medical units of NWCG member agencies and for additional information and updates, please visit the IEMS website at: http://www.nwcg.gov/branches/pre/rmc/iems/index.html.

Incident Emergency Medical Subcommittee

Dental

Triage Priority

Emergency Condition - Transport patient by most rapid, appropriate method available:
- Dental infection causing airway compromise
- Uncontrolled dental or oral bleeding

Urgent Condition - Hospital evaluation, Ambulance transport as needed:
- Dental abscess (infections)
- Dental trauma resulting in avulsed teeth
- Uncontrollable dental pain

Semi-Urgent Condition - Physician evaluation:
- Dental pain (controlled by medications)
- Dry socket

Routine Condition - Medical Unit Treatment:
- Dental caries (cavity) without pain

General:

- The most common cause of dental pain is tooth decay or pulpal disease. Pulpal disease has three phases:
    - Hyperemic - The vascular system responds to an external stimulus, such as dental caries or dental trauma; this is a reversible condition.
    - Pulpitis - The pulp becomes infected
    - Pulpal necrosis - The pulp dies; fluid and pressure build, causing pain
- Therapeutic intervention consists of analgesia and referral to a dentist.

Toothaches

Signs and Symptoms:
- The most common cause of toothaches is pupal disease or dental caries.
- This type of pain is paroxysmal and usually begins with heat and /or cold stimulus. Irreversible pain indicates that the tooth will require either a root canal or extraction.
- This pain usually occurs spontaneously and continues to worsen, especially at night when intracranial pressure builds.
- The tooth becomes extremely sensitive to heat and cold.
- The pain may be reversible if the decay can be removed and the tooth is restored.

Dental - Continued

Toothaches

Treatment:

Routine – Medical Unit evaluation and treatment

- Topical OTC analgesic (eugenol, oil of clove).
- OTC Analgesic – Follow package insert dosage instruction.
- Warm packs to area
- Referral to a dentist if pain persists or infection is present.

Avulsed Teeth

Signs and Symptoms:

- Teeth that have been torn from the mouth by trauma. If found within the first hour the teeth may be implanted.

Treatment:

Urgent – Hospital evaluation

If found within 1 hour and patient is alert and oriented:
- Rinse tooth clean
- Irrigate the wound/socket
- Re-implant the tooth in the original socket
- OTC Analgesic – Follow package insert dosage instruction.

If greater than 1 hour:
- Place the tooth in saline solution
- Check for excessive bleeding from the gums or pulp.
- As these injuries are frequently associated with head injuries, be sure to check the mouth and pharynx area for pieces of the tooth and debris that may obstruct the airway.

Dental - Continued

Dental Abscess

Signs and Symptoms:
- Abscess at the root of the tooth usually resulting from pulpal necrosis, which is a result of caries or trauma.
- Periodontal (recessed pocket between the tooth and gum) abscesses.

Treatment:

Semi-Urgent – Physician evaluation
- These all require dental referral for drainage of abscess.
- Therapeutic intervention consists of drainage of abscess by a dentist.
- Local measures for pain control
  - OTC Analgesic – Follow package insert dosage instruction
  - Warm packs on the area
  - Warm hydrogen peroxide (1.5 %) rinses every 2 hours.
  - If drainage is present, position for drainage out of mouth and be prepared for emesis.

Dry Socket

Signs and Symptoms:
- Dry socket usually occurs 3 - 5 days after tooth extraction, when a blood clot is lost and bone is exposed.

Treatment:

Semi-Urgent – Physician evaluation
- Irrigate socket with saline
- OTC eugenol (oil of cloves) moistened cotton ball packed into the socket.
- OTC Analgesic – Follow package insert dosage instruction.
- Dental referral if pain persists.

Ear

Triage Priority

Emergency Condition - Transport patient by most rapid, appropriate method available:
- Traumatic ear injuries
- Sudden deafness
- Fever above 101.5 F
- Retained foreign bodies with symptoms

Urgent Condition - Hospital evaluation, Ambulance transport as needed:
- Acute tympanic membrane perforation
- Continued ear pain without fever or physical findings
- Patients with underlying illness (e.g. diabetes, multiple medical problems and medications)

General:

There are three requirements for proper ear examination using an otoscope:
- Good illumination
- Magnification
- Patient comfort including adequate physical control of the patient, including proper positioning and sedation

Acute Cellulitis of External Ear
Signs and Symptoms:
- Redness of external ear
- Swelling of external ear
- Tenderness of the external ear
- Fever greater than 101.5 F

Treatment:

Semi-Urgent - Requires physician evaluation

Acute External Otitis
Signs and Symptoms:
- Itching
- Severe ear pain
- Ear tender to touch
- Swelling of the canal
- Infection of the external portion of the ear
- Purulent material in external ear canal

Ear - (Continued)

Acute External Otitis

Treatment:

Semi-Urgent – Physician evaluation
- Fever greater than 101.5
- Hearing loss
- Diabetic or history of multiple medical problems
- Foreign body present in ear canal
- Elderly
- No improvement within two days of treatment.

Acute Otitis Media

Signs and Symptoms:
- Sharp pain inside ear
- History of previous infections
- Antecedent upper respiratory infection
- Hearing loss
- Fever common
- Tympanic membrane red and bulging with landmarks obscured
- Hearing decreased if measured

Treatment:

Semi-Urgent – Physician evaluation

Impacted Earwax

Signs and Symptoms:
- Decreased hearing.
- "Plugged ear".
- Earwax filled ear canal.
- Ear pain is rare in this condition.

Treatment:

Routine – Medical Unit treatment
- Impacted hard wax can be softened for easier removal if patient:
- Use carbamide peroxide, 6.5% (OTC Earwax Removal Kit).

If irrigation is attempted, it should be gentle with a saline irrigating solution at body temperature (100 F). Excessively cold or hot solution causes vertigo.

Ear - Continued

Foreign Body in Ear (including insects)

Signs and Symptoms:
- Diagnosis is obvious with visualization of insect in ear canal.
- Occasionally pain or vertigo (dizziness) may result.

Treatment:

Routine – Medical Unit treatment
- Live insect in the ear canal should be immobilized by suffocation with mineral oil, baby oil (or similar substance).
- Pull the ear lobe gently backward and upward to insert oil.
- After insect is immobile, the ear is flushed with body temperature (100 degree F) saline to remove the insect.
- Attach a short catheter or tube to a 25 - 30 ml syringe filled with body temperature saline. Irrigate as needed, do not advance the catheter beyond the outer margins of the ear.

Note: DO NOT IRRIGATE IF POSSIBLE EAR DRUM DAMAGE.

Excessively cold or hot solutions may cause vertigo.

Physician evaluation as needed

Epistaxis

Triage Priority

Emergency Condition – Transport by the most rapid appropriate method available:

- Unstable patient with signs and symptoms of poor perfusion.
- Patient with severe epistaxis with airway compromise

Urgent Condition - Hospital evaluation, Ambulance transport as needed:
- Uncontrolled continued bleeding

Semi-Urgent Condition - Physician evaluation:
- Recurrent epistaxis
- Controlled epistaxis in patient with underlying medical conditions (anticoagulation, liver disease, patients with hypertension, atherosclerotic heart disease, emphysema)

Routine Condition - Medical Unit Treatment:
- Epistaxis anterior with minor bleeding

General:

- Epistaxis can be anatomically classified as "anterior" or "posterior". The vast majority of epistaxis are anterior. While uncommon, posterior epistaxis can be life threatening due to airway compromise and or uncontrolled bleeding.
- While it is extremely difficult to accurately diagnose anterior and posterior epistaxis in the field, epistaxis which are uncontrolled by direct pressure over the anterior nares (nostrils) with continued significant bleeding in the pharynx are highly suspicious for posterior epistaxis.

Signs and Symptoms:

- Epistaxis is a common emergency complaint.
- Commonly occurs in the following groups:
    - Children
    - Adults 50 –70 years old
    - Patients with blood disease, hypertension or arteriosclerotic heart disease
    - Patients on anticoagulant therapy
    - Alcoholics

Epistaxis - Continued

Treatment:

Urgent – Hospital evaluation

Posterior Epistaxis – Uncontrolled

- Assess and support ABCs
- Sit patient up with neck in slight hyperextension
- Apply direct pressure over involved nares

Routine – Medical Unit treatment

Anterior Epistaxis

- Sit patient up with neck in slight hyperextension
- Lean forward, apply direct pressure over involved nares for 15 minutes
- If bleeding recurs after pressure, is not controlled or involves a patient mentioned above, a physician evaluation is recommended.

Eye

Triage Priority

Emergency Condition - Transport patient by most rapid, appropriate method available:
- Sudden visual loss
- Severe persistent incapacitating eye pain
- Significant trauma to eye or surrounding structures including penetrating injuries of the globe
- Chemical burns
- Patient with known eye conditions with eye complaints
- Acute Glaucoma

Urgent Condition - Hospital evaluation, Ambulance transport as needed:
- Superficial foreign bodies (deep and imbedded and those superficial which do not respond to irrigation – i.e. the patients will still complain of a foreign body sensation in the eye)

Semi-Urgent Condition – Physician evaluation needed:
- Superficial eye infections without loss of vision (red eye and purulent discharge)

General:
- Any eye problems need immediate and prompt attention. Do not hesitate to refer these patients to the physician.
- Always check visual acuity.
- All health care workers should wash their hands before examination of eyes and/or instilling ophthalmic medications.
- Assist with Instillation of OTC or patient's prescription eye medications (drops and ointment)
    - Patient tilts head backward and looks upward
    - Pulls lower lid downward
    - The medication is placed on the conjunctivae of lower lid

Documentation:
- Visual acuity
- Pupil size and reactivity
- Extra ocular eye movement
- Condition and appearance of eyes, lids and surrounding eye structures

Eye - Continued

Superficial eye injuries

Corneal abrasions and or foreign bodies, including contact lens "over wearing" symptoms identical to corneal abrasions and sun induced UV keratitis – "snow blindness".

Signs and Symptoms:

- Foreign body sensation usually with discomfort or pain
- Blurred vision (but not decreased)
- Excessive tearing

Treatment:

Semi-Urgent – Physician evaluation

- If unable to remove foreign body, patient needs to be referred to physician.

Routine – Medical Unit evaluation and treatment

- If superficial foreign body and/or dust, dirt or smoke irritated eye; flush with 250 – 500 ml of sterile saline or clean water.
- Re-examine the patient to see if foreign body has been removed.

Painful red eye

Includes:
- Acute Conjunctivitis
- Acute Iritis
- Acute Glaucoma
- Acute foreign body
- Acute Keratitis

Signs and Symptoms:
- Redness of conjunctivae
- Discharge usually present and may be watery or purulent
- Photophobia (sensitivity to light) usually present

Treatment:

Semi-Urgent

- A physician should evaluate all patients with painful red eyes.

Eye - Continued

Acute Conjunctivitis

Signs and Symptoms:

- Often with history of smoke exposure
- Mild pain or foreign body sensation
- Redness of conjunctiva from inflammation due to irritation or infection.
- Mildly decreased visual acuity
- No history of foreign body
- Eye discharge (watery vs. purulent)
- Prior or current viral symptom (Upper respiratory infection)

Treatment:

Semi-Urgent – Physician evaluation

- Significant pain
- Purulent discharge
- Severe redness
- Any decrease in visual acuity
- Associated medical illness (Diabetes, Glaucoma, etc.)

Gastrointestinal

Triage Priority

Emergency Condition - Transport patient by most rapid, appropriate method available:
- Presence of shock
- Abnormal vital signs
- Severe pain
- Presence of active bleeding (vomiting blood; blood in stool)

Urgent Condition - Hospital evaluation, Ambulance transport as needed:
- History of GI bleeding, with stable vital signs and dark stools (melena).
- Female of childbearing age with any abdominal pain or irregular or missed period
- Moderate recurrent or persistent abdominal pain.
- History of multiple medical problems

Semi-Urgent Condition - Physician evaluation:
- Inability to keep or maintain oral fluid rehydration.

Routine Condition - Medical Unit Treatment:
- Mild abdominal cramps
- Nausea responding to supportive treatment
- Normal vital signs
- No possibility of pregnancy

Acute Gastroenteritis

Signs and Symptoms:
- Diarrhea
- Vomiting
- Fever
- Abdominal pain or cramps
- Blood in stool

Documentation
- Time of onset
- Nature of the symptoms
- Character and amount of vomitus
- Blood in stool
- Fever, chills
- Abdominal pain, character and location
- Pertinent past medical history

<u>Gastrointestinal - Continued</u>

Treatment:

Semi-Urgent – Physician evaluation

- Inability to keep or maintain oral fluid, in spite of attempts at rehydration
- Uncontrolled vomiting

Routine – Medical Unit Evaluation and treatment

- Oral rehydration
  - 32 fl oz, ½ water ½ electrolyte solution (sports drink), slow ingestion over 2-3 hour.
  - Start with small amounts 1–2 teaspoons every few minutes and gradually increase to avoid large amount of fluid collection in the stomach that might cause vomiting.
  - Repeat x 2 until patient is able to urinate.
- Restrict solid food intake.
- Moderate physical activity until signs and symptoms have dissipated.
- For patients with recurring nausea and / or vomiting:
  - OTC antiemetic / antinausea – follow package dosage insert.
- For patients with mild diarrhea, an OTC antidiarrheal if infection is not suspected – follow package dosage instructions.

Gastrointestinal - Continued

Acute Constipation

Signs and Symptoms:

- Hard, infrequent bowel movement
- Patients who are chronically constipated with no underlying illness frequently benefit from an increase in the mass and moisture content of the stools.

Treatment:

Routine – Medical Unit evaluation and treatment

- OTC laxative may have some efficacy. (Use only if abdominal pain is absent)
- Fruits, vegetables and other natural stool softeners (including prunes)
- Increase fluid intake
- Predisposing factors must be recognized and treated. Many medications induce constipation such as codeine & morphine.

Acute Abdominal Pain

Documentation:

- History of pain
  - Time of onset
  - Character, location, severity
  - Female, last menstrual period
  - History of GI bleeding
  - History of GU complaints
  - Past medical history
  - Current medication
- Major age group consideration:
  - Appendicitis
  - Ectopic pregnancy
  - Pelvic inflammatory disease
  - Peptic ulcer disease
  - Infectious gastroenteritis (with cramps)

Treatment:

Urgent – Hospital evaluation
- Assess and monitor ABCs
- Treat for shock as necessary

Genitourinary

Triage Priority

Emergency Condition - Transport patient by most rapid, appropriate method available:

- Presence of shock

Urgent Condition - Hospital evaluation, Ambulance transport as needed:
- Fever greater than 101.5
- Back or rib / flank pain
- Presence of abdominal pain

Semi-Urgent Condition - Physician evaluation:
- Discomfort on urination

Routine Condition - Medical Unit Treatment:
- Vaginitis

Urinary Tract Infection

Signs and Symptoms:

- Burning or pain on urination)
- Urinary frequency
- Discomfort or pain above the pubic area
- Discolored or cloudy urine
- Frequent previous UTI (if patient is female)
- Occasional nausea and vomiting
- Fever greater than 101.5 F
- Tender kidney area, (posterior rib 7 – 12) on light percussion using the side of a closed fist.
- Presence or absence of vaginal discharge

Documentation

- History
- Fever
- Flank pain
- Color of urine

Treatment:
Semi-Urgent – Physician evaluation
- Urinary tract infections require physician consultation.

Genitourinary - Continued

Dysmenorrhea – painful menstruation
Signs and Symptoms:
- Lower abdominal cramping
- Nausea
- Vomiting
- Headache
- Bloating
- Breast tenderness
- Backache
- Fatigue
- Mood changes

These symptoms appear just before (24 – 48 hours) or at the onset of menstruation and are maximal during the first 48 hours afterward.

Gynecologic history should include:
- Age
- Gravidity (total number of prior pregnancies)
- Parity (total number of full term births)
- First day of last menstrual period
- Length and regularity of the cycles
- Duration of flow

Documentation:
- Severity
- Duration
- Character
- Location
- Radiation
- Previous history of painful periods
- Any previous documentation

Treatment:
Semi-Urgent - Physician referral
- New abdominal pain
- Fever greater than 101.5 F
- Severe pain
- Missed period

Routine – Medical Unit evaluation and treatment
- Mild to moderate discomfort
- OTC Analgesic – Follow package insert dosage instruction

Genitourinary - Continued

Vaginitis

Vaginitis is a common and annoying disorder that in absence of other symptoms and signs rarely indicates disease. Common pathogens include *Candida albicans* (yeast infection), *Trichomonas vaginalis*, *Gardnerella vaginalis*.

Signs and Symptoms:

- Vaginal discharge appearance, amount, onset, smell
- Discomfort
- Urinary symptoms (urine may cause discomfort after exiting the urethra and making contact with irritated vaginal mucosa)
- *Candida* usually looks like "cottage cheese", has no odor to it.
- *Trichomonas* and *Gardnerella vaginitis* looks like "dirty dishwater". In particular *Gardnerella* has a "fishy" smell.
- Some patients will have irritation of the skin surrounding the vaginal area.
- Sometimes vaginal discharge is associated with other vaginal infections.

Treatment:

Semi-Urgent – Physician evaluation

- Any signs and symptoms that are out of the ordinary for the patient.

Routine – Medical Unit evaluation and treatment

- Avoid tight fitting garments
- If patient has previous history of "yeast" infection and has discharge consistent with *Candida* (cottage cheese):
  - OTC vaginal antifungal cream – follow package insert dosage instruction.
- If vaginal discharge does not improve by 3 – 5 days or gets worse, have patient referred for evaluation.

Headache

Triage Priority

Emergency Condition - Transport patient by most rapid, appropriate method available:

- Severe headache described as the "worst headache of my life"
- Headache (moderate to severe) with associated:
    - Head trauma, Vision loss, Fever or Altered mental status
- Seizures
- Headache in the setting of toxic gas exposure (carbon monoxide)
- Headache associated with a sustained BP, systolic greater than 200 and / or diastolic greater than 110

Routine Condition - Medical Unit Treatment:

- Mild headache typical for patient and without other symptoms

---

General:

- The presentation of severe headache can be life threatening
- Some life threatening conditions and diseases associated with a severe headache include:
    - Subarachnoid hemorrhage, inter-cranial bleeding, meningitis / encephalitis, severe hypotension with encephalopathy, disorders of oxygenation or respiration (hypoxia, carbon monoxide poisoning).

Signs and Symptoms:

- Severity and onset of pain
- Nature of pain
- Prior history of headache (including migraine)
- History of head trauma
- Mental status
- Vital signs
- Fever
- Neck stiffness

Treatment:

Emergency Condition - Transport patient by most rapid, appropriate method available:

- Assess and support ABCs

Routine Condition

- OTC Analgesic – Follow package dosage instruction
- Re-evaluate in 24 hours or sooner for any change in symptoms.

Insect Stings and Bites

Stings and Bites

Triage Priority

Emergency Condition - Transport patient by most rapid, appropriate method available:

Stings
- With anaphylaxis

Urgent Condition - Hospital evaluation, Ambulance transport as needed:

Stings
- With signs of surrounding tissue infection

Spider Bite
Black Widow bites often result in an immediate and severe reaction within 10-60 minutes.
- Signs / symptoms of poor perfusion.
- Seizures
- Severe pain
- Respiratory distress

Brown Recluse bites may have a delayed reaction time
- With neurological symptoms such as muscle rigidity or tremors.
- Severe pain
- Possible infection

Scorpion Envenomation
- Same as spider bite
- Pain and numbness or prickly, stinging or burning feeling

Semi-Urgent Condition - Physician evaluation:

Spider Bite
- Presence of pustule, or rash.

Scorpion Envenomation
- Local pain and symptoms only

Routine Condition - Medical Unit Treatment:

Stings or Bites
- With only local reactions

Insect Stings and Bites - Continued

Insect Sting

Signs and Symptoms:
- Erythema (redness)
- Pain at site of sting
- Swelling
- Blister
- Cellulitis (swelling and redness)

Treatment:

Routine – Medical Unit evaluation and treatment
- Remove stinger
- Cleanse site
- Apply antiseptic
- Do not apply ice directly to area, use a towel between the skin and ice placed in a plastic bag, (alternate 10 minutes on / 10 minutes off)
- Elevate extremity above the heart
- Consider OTC antihistamines and/or OTC topical steroids – Follow package dosage instructions.

Spider Bite – Brown Recluse

Signs and Symptoms:

Diagnosis:
- The brown recluse spider has a dark, violin shaped area on its back. It is found in old woodpiles, attics, closets, and prefers dark, undisturbed places.

Venom:
- The venom is chiefly cytotoxic, causing local tissue destruction

Clinical Course
- The bite initially seems mild and often goes unnoticed
- Pain begins at the site 1 - 4 hours later, and a red area with a central pustule may be seen
- A typical bull's eye lesion is created when the red blister is encircled by a pale halo with occasional swelling.
- This may turn into a pustule which may gradually grow to form a craterlike lesion over 3 - 4 days, with associated low grade fever
- Healing is often slow and the wound may occasionally require skin grafting

Insect Stings and Bites - Continued

Spider Bite – Brown Recluse

Treatment:

Semi-Urgent – Physician evaluation

- Bites of many other insects (ticks, bedbugs, fleas) can cause small necrotic (tissue death) lesions that may be mistaken for brown recluse spider bite. If uncertain as to the cause of the lesion physician evaluation is needed.
- MRSA (Methicillin Resistant *Staphlococcus aureus*) skin infection can appear like a 'spider bite' with redness and central necrosis, however these patients generally cannot confirm a bite has occurred.

Black Widow Spider

Signs and symptoms

- A few minutes after the bite, a small wheel appears. Many cases do not progress to systemic reactions.
- This may be followed by involuntary muscle spasm resulting in excruciating crampy pain that remains localized or spreads to the thigh, shoulder, back and abdominal muscles.
- Increased severity of symptoms are usually seen in the young or elderly.
- Systemic symptoms include tachycardia, diaphoresis, fever, salivation, vomiting and bronchorrhea (watery sputum).
- Cardiovascular symptoms include hypertension, hypotension (shock) and very rarely cardiac arrest.
- Respiratory symptoms include respiratory muscle weakness, pulmonary edema, respiratory distress.
- Neurological symptoms include weakness, eye droop and seizures.
- Symptoms frequently subside in a few days.

Insect Stings and Bites - Continued

Black Widow Spider

Treatment:

Urgent – Hospital evaluation

- Assess and support ABC's
- Do not apply ice directly to area, use a towel between the skin and ice placed in a plastic bag, (alternate 10 minutes on / 10 minutes off)
- Immobilize the affected extremity.

Scorpion envenomation

General

- The only potentially lethal scorpion is found primarily in Arizona
- Increased severity of symptoms in the very young and elderly. Most patients who are stung have only local reactions; those with neurological symptoms require urgent hospital evaluation.

Signs and Symptoms

- Acute pain, immediately at the sting site.
- Systemic signs:
  - Salivation
  - Diaphoresis (Sweating)
  - Dizziness
  - Shortness of breath
- Cardiovascular:
  - Hypertension
  - Hypotension
  - Pulmonary edema.
- Neurological:
  - Stinging, prickly, or burning feeling
  - Difficulty in swallowing
  - Double vision
  - Involuntary movement of the eyes
  - Visual loss
  - Incontinence
  - Muscle paralysis

Treatment:
Urgent – Hospital evaluation
- Assess and support ABC's

Integument (Skin)

Triage Priority

Urgent Condition - Hospital evaluation, Ambulance transport as needed:

Burns (Full thickness)

General Skin Infections

- If fever or systemic toxicity present

Semi-Urgent Condition - Physician evaluation:

Poison Ivy, Oak, and Sumac

- Significant rash, (face, genitals)

Lacerations

- Lacerations that require suturing
- Lacerations requiring medical evaluation (facial area, genitals, or fingers / toes.

Burns (Partial thickness))

General Skin Infection

- Without fever or signs of systemic toxicity

General Skin Infection

Ingrown Toenail

- With severe pain or signs of infection.

Blisters

- Fever or severe inflammation of the dermal and subcutaneous layers of skin adjacent to the blister.

Routine Condition - Medical Unit Treatment:

Lacerations

- Lacerations, abrasions that do not require suturing

Blister

- If blister present without signs of infection

General:

A delayed hypersensitivity reaction to an oleoresin in these plants

Poison Ivy, Oak, and Sumac

Signs and Symptoms:

- History of exposure to offending plant
- Skin lesions usually in linear streaks corresponding to areas of contact with vines or stems
- Lesions consisting of red patchy areas or linear streaking often with edema or clear vesicles (Blisters).

Integument (Skin) - Continued

Poison Ivy, Oak, and Sumac

Treatment:

Semi-Urgent – Physician evaluation
- For more severe cases (multiple areas on body, swelling and edema of the face or genitals, progressive lesions unresponsive to topical therapy

Routine – Medical Unit evaluation and treatment
- For mild cases, use OTC topical steroid cream or ointment (ointment in dry cracking skin, cream in weeping areas). Follow package application instructions.
- Skin degreaser cleansing agent (dish soap) or OTC Urushiol Oil.
- OTC Antihistamine for itching – Follow package dosage instructions.

Scabies and Lice

General

- Ectoparasitic infestation spread by contact or exposure to contaminated clothing. Most of these parasites survive only a few days away from the hosts.
- Organisms: *Pediculus humanus corporis* (body lice), *capitis* (head lice), *Sarcoptes scabiei* (scabies)
- Clothing should be discarded or washed.
- All contacts need to be treated.

Signs and Symptoms:

- Intense itching
- Scabies mite difficult to see by naked eye. Lice adults and nits can usually be seen in the scalp or genital area.
- General redness and infection of the skin may accompany these lesions.

Treatment:

Semi-Urgent – Physician evaluation and treatment
- Underclothing, bedding and towels should be laundered in hot water to destroy residual organisms.

Integument (Skin) - Continued

Lacerations

General

- Minor lacerations are lacerations that do not require suturing.
- As a general guideline, if the wound can be separated and the underlying fat is visible, the wound will need suturing.
- High-risk lacerations involving eyelids, mouth, genitals, fingers/toes require physician evaluation.

Treatment:

Routine – Medical Unit evaluation and treatment

- All wounds and the surrounding tissue should be cleansed with mild surgical soap and water solution. Do not use iodine-based scrubs on any lacerations.
- Foreign bodies should be flushed and removed if possible.
- The superficial wound should be dressed with an OTC antibiotic ointment and covered with non-adherent gauze pad and tape.
- If steri-strip is needed to close a superficial laceration:
  - Apply a skin prep (benzoin) to adjacent skin and allow to dry
  - Approximate the edges of the wound
  - Apply steri-strip
  - Apply non-adherent dressing and bandage.
- If tetanus status is unknown and cannot be determined, patient requires tetanus. Tetanus status is current if less than 10 years for a clean wound and less than 5 years for a dirty wound.
- Recheck wound in 24 hours.

Integument (Skin) - Continued

Burns

General

- Burns can be classified as partial thickness and full thickness. Any significant burn with lack of sensation (or pain) should be regarded as full thickness.
- The presence of charred skin, blisters, sloughing skin should suggest either significant partial thickness (2nd degree) or full thickness (3rd degree) burn.
- The presence of redness only is suggestive of superficial partial thickness burn

---

Treatment:

Urgent – Hospital evaluation, Ambulance transport as needed

- Major Burns
    - Assess and support ABCs

Semi-Urgent – Physician Evaluation

- Burns with multiple blisters or a single blister that involves more than 1% of body surface (area of patient's palm) require a physician evaluation.

Routine – Medical Unit evaluation and treatment

- Minor Burns (Red skin or blisters that involve less than 1% body surface area.)
    - Evaluate the extent and depth of injury
    - Remove clothing and jewelry. If clothing is adherent to the wound, soak the wound in 1.5% hydrogen peroxide to facilitate removal
    - Relieve pain by applying cool compresses.
    - Ruptured burn blisters – Remove the skin apply OTC topical antibiotic ointment and cover with a dry dressing. Re-evaluate in 24 hours.
    - Intact blisters should be covered with a dry dressing and re-evaluated in 24 hours.
    - The patient should be instructed to keep the dressing cleaned and re-evaluate in 24 hours.
    - The involved extremity should be kept elevated to minimize edema formation
    - Tetanus status must be current or will require a physician evaluation.
    - OTC analgesic – Follow package insert dosage instructions.

Integument (Skin) - Continued

General Skin Infection

General

- Superficial skin infections are usually due to group A streptococci.
- The lesion begins as small vesicles that rapidly blisters and rupture easily.
- The discharge dries, forming the characteristic thick, golden-yellow, stuck on crusts.
- The lesions are painless and often itch
- There is no fever

Treatment:

Semi-Urgent – Physician evaluation

- Criteria for required physician consultation
  - Fever greater than 101.5 F
  - Continued spread in spite of topical OTC antibiotics
  - Red streaks from the site of infection
  - Pain
  - Underlying medical problems such as diabetes.

Ingrown Toenail

Signs and Symptoms:

- Inflammation and infection near a nail fold often due to trauma or sharp edge of the nail

---

Treatment:

Routine – Medical Unit evaluation and treatment

- If possible, snip the sharp edge of the nail off with a small tip scissors.
- If fever, extensive swelling and pain, patient will need physician consult.
- If minor inflammation, clean area with soap and water.
- OTC antibiotic cream, follow package instructions.
- Bandage site.
- Cover with foam dressing as needed
- Recheck patient in 12 hours
- If signs of infection persist a physician evaluation is needed

---

Integument (Skin) - Continued

Blisters

Treatment:

Routine – Medical Unit evaluation and treatment

- Closed
    - Clean area surrounding blister with mild soap and water
    - Apply barrier film and pad area as needed
    - Encourage good foot hygiene
    - Do not open blister unless in an area where friction will recur, then remove blister (dead skin) apply OTC antibiotic ointment as directed by product instructions, cover with a thin dressing and re-check in 12 hours.
- Open
    - Clean area with mild soap and water.
    - Apply OTC antibiotic over open blister
    - Cover with foam dressing
    - Re-evaluate in 12 hours

Athletes Foot

Signs and Symptoms

- Cracks between toes, redness, itching appearance.

Treatment:

Routine – Medical Unit evaluation and treatment

- Good foot hygiene is essential
- Dry feet especially between toes after bathing and rub off scaling skin
- Apply bland drying foot powder, and wear light permeable footwear
- OTC antifungal creams – Follow package application instructions, Treatment may take four to six weeks.
- Physician evaluation for any signs of infection.

Jock Itch

Signs and Symptoms

- Reddened skin around scrotum and thighs. This is a fungal infection secondary to excessive perspiration, itching, chafing and irritation in the groin area. Also check patient for Athletes Foot and treat as needed.

Treatment:

Routine – Medical Unit evaluation and treatment

- OTC antifungal cream or powder – Follow package application instructions.

Musculoskeletal

Triage Priority

Emergency Condition - Transport patient by most rapid, appropriate method available:

- Multiple trauma
- Neurological or vascular compromise
- Signs and symptoms of poor perfusion
- Low Back pain with incontinence (bowel or bladder) or fever
- Open fracture

Urgent Condition - Hospital evaluation, Ambulance transport as needed:

- Obvious dislocation
- Angulation
- Severe pain

Semi-Urgent Condition - Physician evaluation:

- Lower extremity injury: Inability to bear-weight
- Upper extremity injury: Inability to maintain full range of motion
- Significant swelling
- Presence of discoloration and bruising
- Point tenderness

Routine Condition - Medical Unit evaluation and treatment:

Ankle

- Able to walk without a limp
- No tenderness or pain over either side of the ankle
- No tenderness at the base of the foot

Knee

- Able to walk without a limp
- No significant swelling or tenderness

Sprains

Definition:

- Mild Sprain – A ligament that has been stretched
- Moderate Sprain – A ligament that has been partially torn
- Severe Sprain – A ligament that has been completely torn

Mechanism of injury:

- Secondary to force causing stretching, tearing of the ligament involved, the most common sprains are ankles, knees, or shoulders

Musculoskeletal - Continued

Mild (1st degree) Sprain

Signs and Symptoms:

- Slight pain
- Slight swelling

Treatment:

Routine – Medical Unit evaluation and treatment

- Elevation for 12 hours
- Cold pack or ice to area 1st, 24 – 48 hours
- Light weight-bearing
- OTC analgesics – follow medication dosage instructions

Moderate (2nd degree) Sprain

Signs and Symptoms:

- Pain
- Point tenderness
- Swelling
- Inability to bear weight for a short time period.

Treatment:

Semi-Urgent – Physician evaluation

- Splint required.
- Cold pack or ice 48 - 72 hours.
- Elevation for 48 – 72 hours.
- Crutches
- No weight-bearing for 5 - 7 days
- OTC analgesics – Follow medication dosage instructions

Musculoskeletal - Continued

Severe (3rd degree) Sprain

Signs and symptoms

- Pain
- Point tenderness
- Swelling
- Discoloration
- Inability to use
- Instability

Treatment:

Semi-Urgent – Physician evaluation

Sore Muscles and Joints

Signs and symptoms

- Generalized muscle aches and pains caused by overuse and fatigue
- Determine if specific joint is involved

Treatment:

Routine – Medical Unit evaluation and treatment

- OTC analgesics – follow medication dosage instructions

Musculoskeletal - Continued

Acute Low Back Pain

Signs and Symptoms

With mechanical low back pain, the patient will usually have the exact instance causing the pain (i.e., lifting heavy object).

- The patient frequently will have previous history of back strains.
- The patient often complains of dull, deep low back pain that occasionally can radiate into a buttock or leg.
- The pain might be exacerbated by activity and movement and relieved by rest. Other neurological symptoms should be absent.

- Examination of mechanical low back pain reveals decrease flexion and often muscle spasm next to the spine.

Treatment:

Routine – Medical Unit evaluation and treatment

- Rest in position of comfort, ambulate as tolerated
- Ice for 1st 24 hours
- OTC analgesics – follow medication dosage instructions
- No lifting
- Physician evaluation for any of the following;
    - Increasing pain
    - Continued pain after 24 hours.
    - Any numbness, tingling or weakness of the lower extremities.

Respiratory

Triage Priority

Emergency Condition - Transport patient by most rapid, appropriate method available:

- Significant respiratory distress (Rate greater than 30 breaths per minute or, accessory muscle use)
- Signs and symptoms of poor perfusion
- Severe hypoxia (O_2 saturation < 90%)
- Chest pain
- Significant smoke inhalation
- Presence of respiratory burns

Urgent Condition - Hospital evaluation, Ambulance transport as needed:

- Fever greater than 101.5 F
- Mild to moderate hypoxia (oxygen saturation < 90-94% on room air at sea level)
- Moderate respiratory distress (RR between 25-30 breaths / minute)

Semi Urgent Condition - Physician evaluation:

- Severe or persistent cough
- Increased sputum production
- No respiratory distress
- Temperature greater than 100.0 F but less than 101.5 F.

Routine – Medical Unit evaluation and treatment

- Temperature less than 100.0 F)
- Non-productive cough
- No respiratory distress

Note: A pulse oximeter measures the oxygen saturation of hemoglobin. The oxygen saturation is dependent on the amount of oxygen by volume inspired which is dependent on the partial pressure at altitude. As altitude increases the amount of oxygen by volume decreases. This is the 'normal' or expected reading at altitude. However, expect that anyone working at higher altitudes will experience shortness of breath due to the decreased oxygen available until they compensate over time with an increase in the number of circulating red blood cells.

Table 1. Oxygen Saturation at Altitude

Altitude	O_2 Saturation
Sea Level	95-100 %
10,000	88-93 %
13,000	83-88 %
16,000	75-80 %

Respiratory - Continued

Acute Bronchitis

Signs and Symptoms:

- Cough
- Sputum production (clear, green or yellow)
- Malaise or fatigue
- Body aches

Documentation:

- Vital signs
- Severity and duration of cough
- Sputum production (appearance, quantity)
- Absence of chest pain
- Absence of shortness of breath
- Absence of blood in sputum
- Absence of fever
- Absence of other medical illness (asthma, emphysema, etc.)
- Cigarette smoking (amount and number of years)

Treatment:

Semi-Urgent – Physician evaluation

Caution – Any one item requires physician referral:

- Significant dyspnea
- Fever greater than 101.5 F
- Chest pain
- Blood in sputum
- Presence of other medical illness (asthma, emphysema, diabetes, etc.)
- Presence of purulent sputum with fever
- Presence of pulmonary rales (crackles) or wheezing on physical exam

Routine – Medical Unit evaluation and treatment

- Unproductive light to moderate cough without fever and dyspnea
  - OTC cough suppressant / expectorant medications. Follow medication dosage instructions.
- Maintain fluid intake
- Reduce smoke exposure
- Re-evaluate in 24 hours

Respiratory - Continued

Smoke Inhalation

Signs and Symptoms:

- Mild irritation of upper airways and burning pain in the throat and chest
- Dyspnea
- Singed nasal hairs
- Facial burns
- Sputum containing carbon
- Rales or Rhonchi (fine or coarse crackles)
- Wheezes
- Dyspnea
- Cough
- Agitation
- Hoarseness

Documentation:

- Vital signs
- Duration of exposure
- Enclosed space?
- Associated signs of pulmonary burns
- Presence of noxious fumes
- O$_2$ saturation

Treatment:

Emergency Condition - Transport patient by most rapid, appropriate method available:

- Assess and support ABCs
- Any patient with significant potential of serious respiratory burn or smoke inhalation (including carbon monoxide) needs emergent hospital evaluation.

Respiratory - Continued

Acute Asthma

Signs and Symptoms:

- Previous history of "asthma" or reactive airway disease
- Recent inhaler use
- Dyspnea
- Respiratory distress
- Increased respiratory rate
- Accessory muscle use
- Hypoxia
- Wheezing

Table 2. Acute Asthma - Categories of presentation

Presentation	Mild	Moderate	Severe
Color	Normal	Normal	Cyanotic
Mental status	Normal	Normal	May be confused
Speech	Normal	Partial sentence	One to two words
Respiratory rate (breaths / minute)	< 30	30-40	> 40
Diaphoresis	Not present	Occasionally present	Present
Oxygen saturation	>95%	90%-95%	<90%
Wheezes	Occasional	Constant	Severe
Inspiratory/Expiratory	Normal(1:3)	Mildly prolonged	Markedly prolonged

Respiratory - Continued

Acute Asthma

Treatment:

Categorize asthma as mild, moderate or severe per chart.

Emergency Condition - Transport patient by most rapid, appropriate method available:

- Moderate or severe patients.
- Assess and support ABCs

Semi-Urgent – Physician evaluation

- Mild category patients, if symptoms persist, the patient should be transported for definitive treatment and support.

Routine – Medical Unit evaluation and treatment

- Patients who respond to self-medication treatment and meet the following criteria may remain in camp:
  - Normalized respiratory rate (less than 20 breaths per minute)
  - Normal oxygen saturation (greater than 95% saturation at sea level or corresponding value at elevation)
  - Absence of wheezing
  - Absence of respiratory distress
  - Able to speak full sentences without difficulty
- Monitor patient for 1 hour to assure symptoms do not recur
- Reassess several times; at 2, 4 and 6 hours after initial assessment to determine if condition has stabilized.

Snakebites

Triage Priority

Emergency Condition - Transport patient by most rapid, appropriate method available:

- All venomous snakebites

Urgent Condition - Hospital evaluation, Ambulance transport as needed:
- Non venomous snakebites (if positively identified)

General:

- Most snakebites are from nonpoisonous snakes. Among the venomous bites in the USA, 95% are from pit vipers (mostly rattlesnakes)
- Snake venom is a complex mixture of proteolytic enzymes and toxic proteins.
- Early emergency assessment of any snakebite should focus on the wound. Venomous snakes have two fangs that produce deep puncture wounds.
- Extreme pain and discomfort following the bite is suggestive of a venomous bite.
- Non-venomous snakes have rows of small, short teeth that produce bites that look essentially like scratches. The exception being Coral Snakes that may present as small scratches. In Coral Snake habitat all snake bites should have a hospital evaluation.

Signs and Symptoms:

Immediate and early responses

- One or two puncture marks
- Local tissue reactions
    - Edema
    - Discoloration
    - Ecchymosis
    - Pain
- Systemic reactions
    - Hypotension (shock)
    - Tachycardia
    - Diaphoresis can result in a significant envenomation.
    - Nausea
    - Dizziness
    - Weakness

Snakebites - Continued

Treatment:

Emergency Condition - Transport patient by most rapid, appropriate method available:

- Assess and support ABCs
- Immobilize the affected extremity and keep the patient calm.
- Keep affected extremity at the level of the heart and assess the distal pulse to ensure that the arterial circulation has not been occluded.
- Remove all constrictive jewelry.
- Clean wound.
- Identify the snake if possible.
    - Digital pictures are the safest method, most cell phone are capable
    - If you decide to transport the snake, keep in mind that the head of a decapitated snake may exhibit reflex actions as long as 1 hour after being separated from its body, they can still bite. Place snake in a hard-sided container and do not bring in to the medical facility until directed to do so by the facility staff.
- Document time of bite.
- Use a marker to outline initial edema or ecchymosis and note time
- Define and mark an area proximal (above) the bite and measure the circumference every 15 to 30 minutes.
- Rapidly transport the patient to an emergency facility.
- Record vital signs every 15 minutes.
- Do not apply ice or immerse the wound in cold water.
- Do not incise the bite.
- Do not apply suction.
- Do not apply electricity.

Throat

Triage Priority

Emergency Condition - Transport patient by most rapid, appropriate method available:

- Sore throat with airway compromise (i.e. epiglottitis, retropharyngeal abscess)
- Difficulty breathing or respiratory distress
- Trismus (unable to open jaw)

Urgent Condition - Hospital evaluation, Ambulance transport as needed:
- Sore throat
- Hoarseness
- Severe pain on swallowing
- Fever greater than 101.5 F
- Presence of visualized abscess

Semi Urgent Condition - Physician evaluation
- Sore throat with fever
- Exudates
- Tender cervical enlargement or swelling

Routine Condition - Medical Unit Treatment:
- Sore throat with minimal pain and the absence of:
  - Exudates
  - Fever (<102 F)
  - Enlargement of lymph nodes
  - Difficulty swallowing

Documentation:
- Vital signs (including temperature)
- Breathing difficulty
- Appearance of the throat
- Presence of exudates
- Presence of tender pharyngeal anterior cervical swelling
- Absence of difficulty breathing, hoarseness, drooling

Throat - Continued

Acute Pharyngitis

Signs and Symptoms:

- Fever
- Sore throat
- Difficulty swallowing
- Pain referred to ears
- Malaise (fatigue, or feeling of being rundown)
- Headache
- Enlarged tonsils
- Exudates on pharynx or tonsils

Treatment:

Emergency Condition - Transport patient by most rapid, appropriate method available:

- Assess and support ABCs

Semi-urgent – Physician evaluation
- Patients with signs of pharyngitis (redness and exudates)
- Fever greater than 101.5 F
- Patients with history of rheumatic heart fever

Routine – Medical Unit evaluation and treatment
- Patients with minimal pain, no exudates, fever, tenderness or swelling
    - OTC Oral anesthetic lozenges, or spray – Follow medication dosage instructions.
    - Oral Rinse – 1 pint warm water with 1 teaspoon salt, and 1 teaspoon baking soda, (not powder), gargle 3-4 times per day
    - OTC analgesic – Follow medication dosage instructions

Table 3. Cold, Flu, or Allergy

Symptoms	Cold	Flu	Airborne Allergy
Chest discomfort	Mild to moderate	Moderate to severe	Sometimes, Mild
Congestion	Common	Sometimes	Rare
Cough	Common	Sometimes	Sometimes
Duration	3-14 days	Days to weeks	Weeks
Extreme exhaustion	Never	Early and prominent	Never
Fatigue, weakness	Sometimes	Sometimes	Sometimes
Fever	Rare	100-104 F	Never
General aches, pains	Slight	Usual; often sever	Never
Headache	Rare	Common	Sometimes
Itchy eyes	Rare	Rare	Common
Runny nose	Common	Rare	Common
Sneezing	Usual	Sometimes	Usual
Sore throat	Common	Sometimes	Sometimes
Stuffy nose	Common	Sometimes	Common

Table 4. Symptomatic Relief

Symptoms	Category	Common OTC Product
Congestion	Decongestant	Sudafed, Triaminic, Vicks Sinex
Cough	Cough suppressant Expectorant	Robitussin, Vicks Formula 44 Mucinex
Fever	Antipyretic / Analgesic	Aspirin, Tylenol, Aleve, ibuprofen
General aches, pains	Analgesic	Anacin, Tylenol, Excedrin, Advil, Motrin, Aleve
Itchy eyes	Ophthalmic Antihistamine	Allergan, Visine-A, Opcon-A, Alaway
Runny / Stuffy nose	Nasal Decongestant	Afrin, Dristan, Neo-Synephrine, Vicks Sinex
Sore throat	Oral Anesthetic	Cepacol, Cepastat

Glossary

Abscess – A localized collection of Pus surrounded by inflamed tissue.

Advanced EMT (AEMT) – An EMS professional who provides basic and limited advanced life support skills and interventions for patients within the EMS system.

Advanced Life Support (ALS) –Emergency medical care and interventions performed by an Advanced EMT or Paramedic with limited supervision, using critical thinking and autonomous decision making skills which includes invasive procedures and medication administration.

Ambulate – To move from place to place, walk.

Anaphylaxis – Hypersensitivity (as to foreign proteins or drugs) resulting from sensitization following prior contact with the causative agent.

Antiemetic – An agent that reduces or prevents vomiting.

Arteriosclerotic - A chronic disease characterized by abnormal thickening and hardening of the arterial walls with resulting loss of elasticity.

Basic Life Support (BLS) – Emergency medical care and interventions performed by an EMT with minimal equipment, limited medications and non-invasive procedures.

Cellulitis - Diffuse and especially subcutaneous inflammation of connective tissue.

Certification – Generally, recognition by the private sector of a nongovernmental and voluntarily achieved standard.

Conjunctivitis – inflammation of the conjunctiva.

Dental Caries – A progressive destruction of bone or tooth; *especially*: tooth decay.

Dry Socket – A tooth socket (aka. cavity) in which after tooth extraction a blood clot fails to form or disintegrates without undergoing organization; *also* : a condition that is marked by the occurrence of such a socket or sockets and that is usually accompanied by neuralgic pain but without suppuration.

Ecchymosis - The escape of blood into the tissues from ruptured blood vessels marked by a livid black-and-blue or purple spot or area; *also*: the discoloration so caused (aka. bruise).

Ectoparasite – A parasite that lives on the exterior of its host.

Edema - An abnormal excess accumulation of serous fluid in connective tissue or in a serous cavity—called also *dropsy.*

Efficacy – The power to produce an effect.

Emergency Medical Technician (EMT) - An EMS professional who provides basic life support skills and interventions for patients within the EMS system.

Encephalitis – Inflammation of the brain.

Encephalopathy – A brain dysfunction from trauma, or other metabolic condition.

Epiglottitis - Inflammation of the epiglottis.

Epistaxis – Nosebleed.

Erythema - Abnormal redness of the skin due to capillary congestion (as in inflammation).

Expanded Scope of Practice- Skills and interventions not included in the *National EMS Scope of Practice Model* necessary for EMS professionals functioning in health care settings other than typical pre-hospital emergency care including, but are not limited to, emergency departments, physician's offices, urgent care settings, occupational medicine, summer camps, wildland fire medical units, disasters, etc.

Exudate - Exuded matter; *especially* : the material composed of serum, fibrin, and white blood cells that escapes from blood vessels into a superficial lesion or area of inflammation.

Glaucoma - A disease of the eye marked by increased pressure within the eyeball that can result in damage to the optic disk and gradual loss of vision.

Hemodynamic – Relating to or functioning in the mechanics of blood circulation.

Incontinence - Inability of the body to control the evacuative functions e.g., urine or fecal *incontinence.*

Iritis - Inflammation of the iris of the eye.

Keratitis - Inflammation of the cornea of the eye characterized by burning or smarting, blurring of vision, and sensitiveness to light and caused by infectious or noninfectious agents—called also *corneitis.*

Licensed Physician – A physician licensed by a state Board of Medicine to practice medicine or surgery in that state.

Licensure – The permission granted by a state as a property right to an individual to practice a profession.

Medical Director – A physician responsible for the oversight of the EMS system, EMS agencies and licensed EMS personnel WITHIN A SPECIFIC GEOGRAPHICAL AREA.

Meningitis - 1: Inflammation of the meninges and especially of the pia mater and the arachnoid , 2: A disease that may be either a mild illness caused by any of numerous viruses (as various coxsackieviruses) or a more severe usually life-threatening illness caused by a bacterium (especially the meningococcus or the serotype designated B of *Haemophilus influenzae*), that may be associated with fever, headache, vomiting, malaise, and stiff neck, and that if untreated in bacterial forms may progress to confusion, stupor, convulsions, coma, and death.

National Association of State EMS Officials – The lead organization for developing national EMS policy and oversight, providing vision, leadership and resources for the improvement of state, regional and local EMS and emergency care systems.

National Registry of EMTs (NREMT) – A national organization that ensures graduates of EMS educational programs have met minimal standards by measuring competency through a uniform testing process.

National Scope of Practice Model - The *National EMS Scope of Practice Model* published by the National Highway Traffic Safety Administration defines and describes four levels of EMS licensure: Emergency Medical Responder (EMR), Emergency Medical Technician (EMT), Advanced EMT (AEMT), and Paramedic. Each level represents a unique role, set of skills, and knowledge base.

Oleoresin - A natural plant product (as copaiba or turpentine) containing chiefly essential oil and resin.

Orthostatic – Of, relating to, or caused by erect posture.

Otitis - Inflammation of the ear.

Over The Counter (OTC) Medications – Drugs that can be purchased without a prescription.

Paramedic - An EMS professional who provides basic and advanced life support skills and interventions for patients within the EMS system.

Paroxysmal – Of, relating to or marked by paroxysms (the hypertension may be either sustained or *paroxysmal).*

Photophobia - Intolerance to light; *especially*: painful sensitiveness to strong light.

Purulent – Containing, consisting of, or being pus (a *purulent* discharge or a *purulent* lesion), accompanied by suppuration (*purulent* meningitis).

Retropharyngeal – Situated, or occurring behind the pharynx such as *retropharyngeal* abscess.

Scope of Practice – A predefined set of skills, interventions or other activities that an EMS professional is legally authorized to perform when necessary, usually set by state law or regulation and local medical direction.

Standard of Care - Conduct exercising the degree of care, skill, and judgment that would be expected under like or similar circumstances by a similarly educated, reasonable EMS professional.

Triage - The sorting of patients (as in an emergency room) according to the urgency of their need for care.

Tympanic Membrane – A thin membrane separating the middle ear from the inner part of the external auditory canal that vibrates in response to sound energy and transmits the resulting mechanical vibrations to the structures of the middle ear—called also *eardrum, tympanum.*

Vaginitis – Inflammation (as from bacterial or fungal infection, allergic reaction, or hormone deficiency) of the vagina that may be marked by irritation and vaginal discharge.

Vesicles - A small abnormal elevation of the outer layer of skin enclosing a watery liquid.